W9-AVJ-148

Before I Sleep

Nov 12, 2015

To LUKE AND OLIVER

SWEET DREAMS

IN

YOUR NEW BEDROOM

LOVE,

RICKY

Before I Sleep

poems for children who think

Samuel Barondes

Illustrated by **Mark Wooding**

North Street Steps Press

Copyright © 2014 by Samuel Barondes

North Street Steps Press

Sausalito, California 94965

All rights reserved

ISBN-13: 978-0615962917

ISBN-10: 0615962912

Library of Congress Control Number 2014908002

Permission to reproduce selections from this book should be addressed to:

North Street Steps Press

425 Bridgeway

Sausalito, CA 94965

For Jonah, Ellen and Asher

CONTENTS

To the Reader

When a child prepares for bed
And a story will be read
You may wish to take the time
To include a little rhyme

One designed to entertain
And inspire a growing brain
Helping it to figure out
What the world is all about.

And if you would like to see
Samples of such poetry
Here are some I hope will please,
Why not start with one of these.

Before I Sleep

When my story has been read,
And the goodnights have been said,
Thoughts keep flowing in my mind
As I leave the day behind.

Mostly I review my day,
Happenings that came my way,
Things I'd finished or begun,
Other things I might have done.

Sometimes I then turn to me,
Who I hope some day to be,
If I'm really who I seem,
Plans to work on when I dream.

Then, when no more thoughts arise,
Time has come to close my eyes,
Fluff the pillow for my head,
Snuggle up and go to bed.

Class Picture

My hair is combed, my shirt is pressed,
My classmates all are neatly dressed,
And I am standing near one end
With Annabelle, my closest friend,

And there is Jena next to Zach,
Jimmy, Julianne, and Jack,
Having chosen favorite places,
Squeezing smiles on childish faces,

Not knowing how it came to pass
We came together in this class,
Not knowing the big role each played
In shaping others in our grade,

And unaware that through the years
We'd find this photo of our peers,
Single out some special member,
And cherish what we can remember.

My Teddy

I don't know why I love him,
I've picked off all his fluff,
His body's gotten dirty,
His feet have gotten rough.

An arm had started hanging,
One morning it was gone,
We found it in my blanket
And my mother sewed it on.

He started leaking stuffing
And my father had a thought:
Let's get ourselves a new one
At the store where he was bought.

But I preferred to patch him
As he gradually became
More worn, and torn, and tattered,
Since his soul still stayed the same!

And as I've gotten older
I keep him on a shelf
Inside a little basket
I made in school — myself.

And if I'm sad and lonely
Or something seems amiss,
I take him down and hug him
And we have a little kiss.

My Thumb

Whenever I was feeling glum
I'd cuddle up and suck my thumb
And choose sweet thoughts to think about
With my blankie, or without.

But as the time arrived for school
I realized it wasn't cool,
Since even I already knew
It's not what kindergartners do.

And so I did it just at night
Although I knew it wasn't right,
Then step-by-step did less and less
Till, finally, complete success.

And now when I observe a kid
Who sucks his thumb the way I did
I think of all that I went through
When I was small and did it too.

The Slide

In my park there is a slide
To which we all return
And get into a little line
So each can take her turn.

And everybody seems to know
She cannot jump ahead
Holding back the others
So she can slide instead.

And if somebody cuts in line
The rest of us protest
Insisting she must wait her turn
Along with all the rest.

This seems to be the fairest way
By which we all decide
Who is first and who is next
When going down the slide.

Baddies

Most fairy tales that I have heard
Have someone who is mean:
A wicked witch, a big bad wolf,
An evil king or queen.

And when the good defeat the mean,
Which always makes me glad,
I've often asked my mother
If real people are this bad.

She said there aren't many
But I should be aware
That though the good outnumber them
Some baddies are out there.

And if I don't watch out for them
I'll take it on the chin
Since life is not a fairy tale:
The good don't always win.

Flowers

It seems that everybody knows
The kind of flower called a rose
And I am pretty sure that some
Can point out a chrysanthemum.

But do you recognize the face
Of cyclamen, or Queen Anne's lace?
And is that flower on the hill
A dahlia or a daffodil?

You still can like a flower's smell
Though what it's called you cannot tell,
And you can like its color too
Although it isn't known to you.

But since my dad taught me the art
Of telling all the flowers apart
The way I see them's not the same:
I know them, now, like friends, by name.

Our Tree

Our playground tree had fallen down
As wind and rain swept through the town
Removing all the welcome shade
Beneath its branches where we played.

Then workmen came with power saws,
And tractors with large metal claws,
To cut our fallen tree apart
And haul its pieces in their cart.

But soon the workmen all came back
With several young trees on a rack,
Took each of them out of its pot
And planted it around this spot.

So now we watch these new trees grow
And all of us are pleased to know
That they're a tribute from the town
To our old friend who'd fallen down.

At the Playground

At the playground I can find
Little kids of every kind,
So I look around to see
Whom I'd like to play with me.

I have learned some ways to tell
Kids I'll get along with well,
Kids who make me feel that they're
Happy, friendly, fun, and fair.

And I've learned that others too
Try to pick the way I do,
Finding ways they can detect
Signs of playmates to select.

So it doesn't take too long
Sorting right ones from the wrong,
Choosing kids with whom to play
And those from whom to stay away.

Picking Your Nose

Don't pick your nose in public,
Don't pick it at your school,
Don't pick it at the drugstore,
Don't pick it at the pool.

Don't pick it at the movies,
Don't pick it at the mall,
Don't pick at a track meet,
Or while you're playing ball.

And if your nose needs picking
Since something in it's sticking,
Make sure that no one spied it —
Then find a place to hide it.

Too Many Teddies

Jack's room is full of teddies,
They clutter up the floor,
They take up all his shelf space,
They're crammed in every drawer.

His desk is overflowing,
His chairs each hold a heap,
His bed contains so many
He has no place to sleep.

He used to search for teddies
At every teddy store
But now he's put the word out:
"I don't want any more."

So if a person brings one
He says, "Please take it back!
I have two hundred teddies
And I'm just a single Jack."

Choices

I'm at a birthday party
Standing by the cake,
The table's filled with goodies,
Which I am free to take.

I see so many choices
I don't know where to start,
I reach out for a creampuff,
Then spot a lemon tart.

There are Snickers, chocolate kisses,
Abba Zabbas, Twix, and gummies,
Tootsie Rolls and dark mint patties
In a bowl with other yummies.

It seems unfair to have to choose
Among the treats I love,
And so I quickly stuff my plate
With all of the above.

Chess

My team is lined up for the fight,
My pieces are all painted white,
With pawns in front of the attack
The other pieces in the back.

I take them from their starting spaces
And move them to more useful places,
Setting traps while making sure
That my positions are secure.

All the while I have a plan
And always do the best I can
To stick to it and figure out
How to bring the plan about,

While black team tries to do the same
By making moves to win the game,
As each of us tries to detect
The moves that we did not expect.

And that's why chess is so much fun,
Because when a good game is done,
The two of us have learned a lot
Though one has won, and one has not.

A Very Hard Call

The batter hit the baseball
He hit it in the air
He hit it down the foul line
He thought the ball fell fair.

The umpire tracked it carefully,
His face froze in a scowl,
He said it crossed the foul line
Which meant the ball fell foul.

He might have been mistaken,
It happens to us all,
A ball that falls beside the line
Is sometimes hard to call.

So when you hit a close one
It means you must prepare
To have the ball you hit called foul
Although it may be fair.

Brain Dials

There is a dial inside my brain
That turns to make me sad,
It sits beside another dial
That turns to make me glad.

I'd like to learn to grab them
And turn them up or down
To give myself a joyful smile
And take away a frown.

But every time I reach in
The dials just seem to hide.
I've never learned to find them:
My brain's too dark inside.

Paper Boats

I made a boat from paper
I put it in my tub
I watched it float around me
As I had a little scrub.

And then I made another
Out of paper I could get
That isn't so absorbent
So it wouldn't get so wet.

Soon I had a dozen
Each in the same shape
But with different markings
Made with different colored tape,

Floating in the bathtub
Between the hands and feet
Of the builder and commander
Of my splendid paper fleet.

Halloween

On Halloween what I like most
Is getting dressed up like a ghost
By putting on a big white sheet,
Which drapes around my head and feet,

So once I'm covered none can see
That underneath the sheet is me,
And none can tell that I am who
Is doing things I rarely do,

Like following my friends around
While giving off a ghostly sound,
Enjoying how they all react
When I put on this ghostly act.

And while I'm having so much fun,
By entertaining everyone,
I'm also pleased they pay me back
By filling up my candy sack.

Healing

When I was climbing up a tree
I hit a branch and scraped my knee,
Which bled so much I was afraid,
And sorry for the mess I'd made.

But soon a scab had formed a seal
Atop the scrape so it could heal,
And growth kept happening within
To fill the scrape with healthy skin,

Till all was healed, as good as new,
Though no one told me what to do,
And all was done so perfectly,
Though none of it was up to me.

Like arguments with friends I've had,
Which seemed at first to be so bad,
But really weren't a big deal—
If they were just allowed to heal.

Correcto

I have a friend who has a way
Of letting someone know
He's in complete agreement
By ending "correct" with an "O."

It shows that he's excited,
It let's his feeling flow.
"Correct" just seems too boring,
"Correcto" says "it's so!"

And I have learned to copy him
In adding that one letter.
When I elect to say "correct,"
"Correcto" is much better.

Scary Stories

I hate a scary story
Before I go to bed.
I hate the one where the boy and the girl
Leave a trail with some crumbs of bread.
And the birds eat the crumbs, and the children are lost,
Till they find a gingerbread shed.
And they think they're safe, but a witch lives there,
So they're really in danger instead.

And I hate the one where a little girl
Wants to bring her grandma a treat,
But a wolf sneaks into the grandma's bed
And hides himself under her sheet,
Then tries to deceive the little girl
By making believe he's sweet,
When all he's after is eating her up
Like a piece of hamburger meat.

I hate these scary stories
For the scary message they send.
Please tell me a happy story
With a very happy end!

Free Throw

The player kicked me in the leg
As I jumped for the ball,
It made me lose my balance
And caused a nasty fall.

This brought me to the foul line,
Entitled to a shot,
When I began to question
"Would I get it in— or not?"

And that's when I remembered
That being in the clutch,
My coach had made me promise
I wouldn't think too much,

And if I had that question
I really shouldn't ask it,
So I just bounced the basketball,
And shot it through the basket.

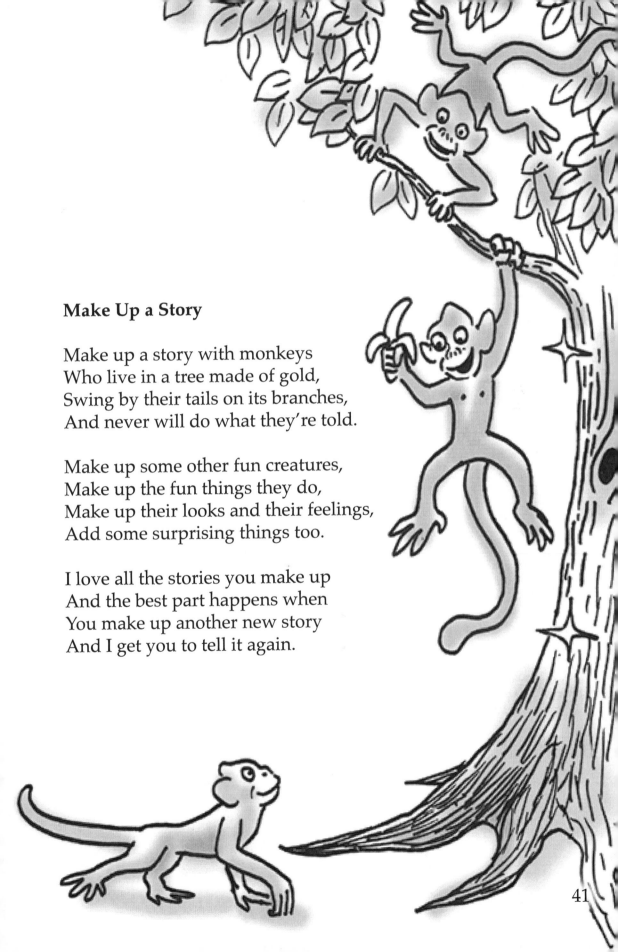

Make Up a Story

Make up a story with monkeys
Who live in a tree made of gold,
Swing by their tails on its branches,
And never will do what they're told.

Make up some other fun creatures,
Make up the fun things they do,
Make up their looks and their feelings,
Add some surprising things too.

I love all the stories you make up
And the best part happens when
You make up another new story
And I get you to tell it again.

Sand Castles

I built a castle out of sand
With shells and other things at hand,
I built it on a strip of beach
I thought the waves would never reach.

I built two towers, tall and round,
I covered them with stones I'd found,
And when the time had come to stop
I put a little flag on top.

And then I had a bad surprise:
The tide began to rise and rise,
Which filled me with increasing fear
As giant waves kept getting near,

Then started a big wave attack
By leaping to the castle's back
And tearing down the castle wall,
Which made the mighty towers fall,

Till all was gone but saddened me,
Who fled the power of the sea,
While learning things may fall so fast
If we don't work to make them last.

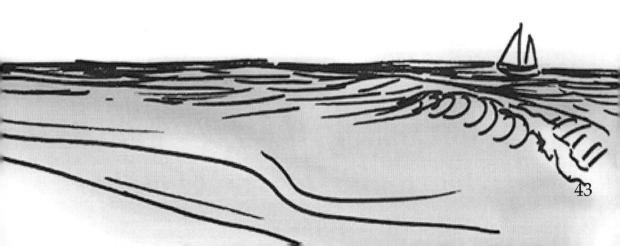

Thinking

Once I've decided to do
A task that's entirely new
I try not to ask
How to do the new task
Instead I start thinking it through.

The process I use is designed
To let thoughts just pop into mind,
They come willy-nilly
And many are silly
I never know just what I'll find.

The thoughts I come up with are fun
But they must be checked one by one.
I propose and reject,
See what's wrong, what's correct,
Until the thought process is done.

I'm pleased I can bring this about
And know I can't do it without
Taking time to imbed
A rough plan in my head
But how, I just can't figure out.

Puzzled, I've tried now and then
To discuss this with very wise men
Who say that "the brain
Is too hard to explain,
But we're sure you can do it again."

Advice

My father said: "dig in your heels,
Stand firm and hold your ground!
Always stick to your ideals,
And don't get pushed around!"

My mother had a different view,
She said that I would find
A lot of situations
Where I must change my mind.

As I grew up I realized
The best advice I've had
Is sometimes think like mother,
And sometimes think like dad.

Back to School

Summer days begin to cool,
Soon I'm going back to school,
Eager as the time draws near
To begin another year.

Getting shoes in bigger size,
Stocking up on school supplies,
Filling backpack with new books,
Pens and pencils in their nooks.

Looking back on months of fun,
Thankful for the things I've done,
I'm excited to return,
There's so much I want to learn.

And excited when I see
Yellow busses come for me,
Happy as the summer ends
Riding back to school with friends.

Feeling Colors

If feeling blue
Means feeling sad,
And feeling black
Feels very bad,

I think the shade
For feeling mellow
Is bright and sunny:
Feeling yellow.

Tests

Tests used to make
My stomach ache.
I'd lie awake
My hands would shake.
I feared I'd make
A dumb mistake!

But now I find that tests are fun.
Can't wait to take another one.
The secret: Get my homework done!

At the Grocery

I wish I could thank
The people who bake
My bread and my muffins,
My rolls and my cake.

I wish I could thank
Those who cook up the pans
Of soup and spaghetti
And put them in cans.

I wish I could thank
Those who grow my potatoes,
My apples and grapes,
My corn and tomatoes.

But all of them seem
To be hiding themselves
Somewhere behind
The big grocery shelves.

The Makeitup Bird

The makeitup bird
Has a make it up trick,
He makes up fun words,
He makes them up quick.

He makes some for kids
Like boogers and snot,
And some I won't mention,
And some I cannot.

He makes some for grownups
Like geek and pizzazz,
Schmooze, mumbo jumbo,
And razzamatazz.

So please give him thanks
For words that amuse
And add bright new color
To language we use.

Since chances are good
If their sound seems absurd
That each was made up
By the makeitup bird.

Reading Minds

A mother keeps trying
To read her child's mind
And figure out what to expect.

She starts by relying
On clues that she finds
When her eyes and his eyes connect.

But clues he's supplying
About how he feels
Are frequently hard to detect.

So thoughts she's applying
To figure him out
Are likely to be incorrect.

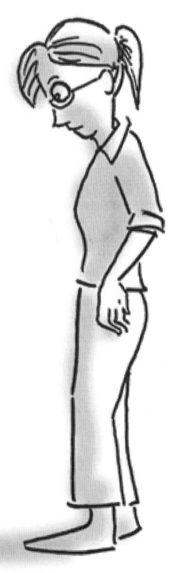

Grandpa's Attic

In grandpa's attic I can see
Bits of family history
And many things that he'd enjoy
When he was just a little boy.

Although he's old I guess I knew
He played with toys I play with too:
A checkers set, a baseball bat,
A wooden sled, a cowboy hat.

Yet seeing them with my own eyes
I began to realize
Though much has changed from him to me
There's also continuity.

And since the attic helps me see
These signs of similarity
For now I cannot get enough
Of grandpa showing me his stuff.

Computer Game

One key moves him forward,
Another moves him back,
A third one is for jumping
Away from an attack.

And as I keep on practicing
And learning key control
My guy keeps getting better
At moving to his goal.

It's gotten to the point that
I get the highest score,
Have reached a record level,
And can't win any more.

So mommy says to move on
But I cannot agree
To say goodbye
To my little guy
Who likes to play with me.

Math Class

It isn't hard to calculate
That three plus five adds up to eight,
And I don't need a bag of tricks
To know that two times three is six.

But learning math gives me the tools,
The ways of thinking and the rules,
I simply cannot be without
When I am asked to figure out

Problems I can't understand
By counting fingers on my hand,
And ones where I don't know each fact
But seek an answer that's exact.

For math allows my mind to play
And look at things another way,
To find what I may not expect
And know the answer is correct.

Air

The air I breathe I cannot see
While it goes in and out of me
And I am told I take it in
Because it has some oxygen.

I take it in without a thought
Since something in me says I ought
To get the oxygen from air
Although I didn't know it's there.

And there are other things I do
For reasons that I never knew
While lots of things go on in me
In ways that are a mystery,

Like dreams that pop into my mind
Whose origins I cannot find
And come and go from who knows where
In and out—just like the air.

Patty is Chatty

My teammate named Patty
Is always so chatty
She just doesn't know when to stop.

She jibbers, she jabbers,
She constantly blabbers,
Her stories are over the top.

There must be a way
To break in and say
Her continuous talk is a flop.

If her prattle persists
I may not resist
Telling Patty to kindly shut up.

Rules

Some rules are made to be followed:
Rules that were nicely designed
To teach you to think before acting
Then help you to make up your mind.

Some rules are made to be broken:
Rules that will stand in your way
Painting just black and white choices
When so many choices are gray.

So as you grow up keep on learning
Ways not to make the mistake
Of breaking the rules you should follow
And following the rules you should break.

A Monkey

I saw a monkey at the zoo
Who swung down from a tree
Looked at me directly
And stuck his tongue at me.

I found it so amusing
To see this tongue attack
I pushed my own tongue forward
And did the same thing back.

This may have pleased the monkey
Although it's hard to know
The signs of satisfaction
That little monkeys show.

And then we eyed each other
As we both stayed in our places:
Two funny little creatures
Who'd made funny little faces.

My Doctor

My doctor checks my height and weight
And asks what foods I like and hate,
She shines a light into my eyes
And asks how much I exercise.

She glances at my ears and nose,
My neck, my fingers, and my toes,
Then slyly asks me if I smoke
(She likes to make a little joke).

She tells me I'll avoid disease
With vitamins from As to Ds,
And then I get a needle stick
With vaccine so I won't get sick.

And when she's done she shakes my hand
While asking if I understand
What I should do and I should stop,
Then lets me choose a lollipop.

Gobbledygook

Gobbledygook, gobbledygook,
I saw the word in a library book,
Stared at its letters to have a good look,
But I couldn't figure out gobbledygook.

My teacher explained it refers to a phrase
That's long and confusing in so many ways
You can't comprehend what idea it conveys
And thinking about it just makes your eyes glaze.

Now I can recognize gobbledygook:
When somebody speaks and I take a close look,
But can't understand what position he took,
I'll know what he's saying is gobbledygook.

First Snow

How I loved that winter day
When mommy taught me how to play
In mounds of freshly fallen snow
All bundled up from top to toe.

As snowflakes fell she took me out
And showed me how to walk about
By making sure that I would keep
My feet from sinking in too deep.

She put a ski cap on my head
And pulled me on a wooden sled
And even let me have the thrill
Of sliding down a little hill.

And once the sledding had been done
Our giant snowman was begun
With stones for eyes and carrot nose,
A hat and scarf his only clothes.

This took so long the day grew old,
And seeing I was getting cold
We went back home to warm me up
With blankets and a cocoa cup.

And as my icy fingers thawed
I clapped my hands so they'd applaud
A day to keep in memory
Of mommy's winter play with me.

Mistakes

Mistakes often go to a red box
That's tucked in the depths of your brain
And once they have gotten inside it
Give rise to emotional pain.

Mistakes that get into the red box
Can keep you from sleeping at night
By finding harsh words to remind you
Your actions just weren't all right.

Mistakes also go to a green box,
A much less emotional place
That doesn't give rise to bad feelings
Like shame and regret and disgrace.

Instead there are tools in the green box
To view a mistake and think through it
Then offer suggestions that show you
How next time you won't have to do it.

So should you keep making some slip ups
Don't let your anxiety spread.
Just open the lid to the green box
And hold down the lid to the red.

What If

What if I were born a Greek
Or Thai or Portuguese?
What if I were raised to speak
Dutch or Japanese?

What if I were brilliant
Or exceptionally tall?
What if I were popular
Or good at basketball?

What if there had been a change
In when I was alive?
What if my first birthday
Was in 1365?

It's fun to have these "what ifs"
That pop into my head
And turn me from familiar me
To someone else instead.

A Monster

Is there a monster in my house?
If so it isn't fair
For him to keep on hiding,
I've hunted everywhere.

It's not that I like monsters
But if he is around
It would be more polite of him
To let himself be found.

So show yourself, mean monster!
And if you don't obey
I'll know that I imagined you,
And make you go away.

The Children I Meet

The children I meet
Are a very mixed lot.
Some are friendly
Others not.

Some are fair,
Some are greedy,
Some are grateful,
Some are needy,

Some are grumpy,
Some are cool,
Some are loving,
Some are cruel.

Each thinks thoughts
I cannot see.
How come they're
Not all like me?

Rock, Paper, Scissors

A rock can smash a scissors
With heavy crashing shots
While paper brushes off rock's blows
And ties rock into knots.

Yet paper can't defend itself
From scissor's stabs and slits,
Which pick apart poor paper
Into tiny little bits.

So in a world of challenges
The safest thing to do
Is build your inner scissors
And your rock and paper too.

The Bird

I heard a thump against my house,
Which made me look outside,
And there, beneath my window,
A baby bird had died.

He'd wanted to fly in to me
But didn't see the glass,
Instead he bumped right into it
Expecting that he'd pass.

And so my dad and I went out
To dig a little hole
In which we put the birdie
With blessings for his soul,

Then, having covered him with leaves,
My daddy took my hand
And said that from this sadness
He hoped I'd understand,

That some day I might come upon
Things I too may not see,
Just like the glass that killed the bird
Who tried to fly to me,

And that my best protection
Is the knowledge I'll amass
To help me figure out how I
Won't bump into the glass.

Hatching

The egg was bouncing
Bump, bump, bump,
The chick inside went
Thump, thump, thump,

His beak began to
Chip, chip, chip,
His shell began to
Rip, rip, rip,

His head popped up to
Peep, peep, peep,
While softly singing
Cheep, cheep, cheep,

And when he finished
Being born,
I fed him
Tiny bits of corn.

A Goldfish

I have a little goldfish
Who is my favorite pet,
She doesn't make much trouble
She never gets upset.

She always seems so happy
Fulfilling her one goal
Of swimming round in circles
Inside her shiny bowl.

I like to keep her near me
On the shelf beside my bed,
Have learned to change her water,
And to make sure she is fed.

I find her so appealing
I hope you too will get
A lovely little goldfish
If you haven't got one yet.

Seeds

I got some seeds from daddy,
Put them in a pot,
Set it on my windowsill
In a sunny spot,

Watched as bright green leaves appeared
Reaching for the sun,
Watched the stalks come out of them
Rising one by one,

Saw the buds pop open
Until they had become
A bunch of yellow daisies,
And gave them to my mom.

This pleased my mom so much that she
Plucked a little pair,
Smiled at me so lovingly,
And put them in her hair.

Ice Cream Cone

My ice cream cone begins to melt
The moment that I get it
And as the drips begin to grow
I try ways to not let it.

I find that what works best for me
Is eating really fast,
That way there's not much dripping
From the first lick to the last.

This works well with a single scoop,
But if I get a double,
I may not eat it fast enough
To put off melting trouble.

So then I change my eating plan
To one I can control:
I take the ice cream, cone and all,
And eat it from a bowl.

Making Cookies

I like to make some cookies,
I mix them all from scratch,
With crunchy little nuggets
In every single batch.

But I get tired of waiting
While all the cookies take
Their time inside the oven
To bake, and bake, and bake.

It seems like an eternity
For baking to get done
And cookies to get cool enough
To eat them one by one.

So while I wait I have a treat
Whose baking doesn't matter,
I lick the bowl I mixed them in
Of all remaining batter.

Make Believe

Make believe you're a wizard,
Make believe you're a witch,
Make believe that you're famous
And incredibly rich.

Make believe you're a hero,
Make believe you're a star,
Make believe you're an expert
On electric guitar.

Make believe that you're different,
Sometimes different is fun.
Make believe has no limits
You can be anyone.

And should things go badly,
There's no need to grieve:
It's only imagined,
It's just make-believe.

Mosquito

In the middle of the night
I woke with a mosquito bite
And heard the buzzing in my ear,
Which meant the insect was still near.

Afraid more biting was ahead
I pulled the covers of my bed
To make a place where I could hide
Beneath my blanket when he tried.

I know mosquitoes have to feed
By piercing skin to make it bleed
While other insects, like the ants,
Are happy eating leafy plants.

And then I had a dream that he
Would lose his appetite for me,
Stop circling round my sleepy head,
Go out and bite a leaf instead.

Magic

I like to watch magicians
Who fill me with surprise
By making rabbits disappear
Right before my eyes.

I know it's not true magic,
It's just a clever scheme
To build a world of make believe
That's not what it may seem.

But there are times when make believe
Really hits the spot.
It lets me feel that magic's real,
Even though it's not.

Jungle Gym

There's a place in the Jungle Gym
I find too hard to climb,
The others are so easy
I climb them all the time.

There's a place in the Jungle Gym
That always seems too high,
The others are so reachable
I hardly have to try.

My mother keeps on telling me
I needn't feel distress,
I'll grow a few more inches
And that will bring success.

But I keep trying new ways
And do not plan to stop.
Its fun to seek a new technique
To climb up to the top.

Sensitive Sue

Sensitive Sue
Didn't know what to do
When she felt that she'd been offended.

She thought our friend Jean
Had said something mean,
Though that's not what Jean had intended.

When Jean said to Sue
What she thought wasn't true
Sue's feelings were rapidly mended.

Then Sue felt less tense,
And stopped taking offense,
And that's how her troubles were ended.

A Lipstick

Stacey saw a lipstick
On mommy's bathroom shelf
And wondered what would happen
If she put it on herself.

She gazed into the mirror
Above the bathroom sink
And carefully applied some
Until her lips were pink.

She studied her reflection
Examining the change
And thought that with the lipstick
Her face seemed awfully strange.

So Stacey took a tissue
And wiped it all away
Then switched right back to childhood
And ran outside to play.

One World

There's a girl in my class from Nigeria,
Another who moved here from Spain,
Her mom is Chinese,
Her dad's Japanese,
Her grandpa was born in Ukraine.

There's a boy on my team from Australia,
Another was raised in Peru,
Our pitcher's Rumanian,
Our catcher's Albanian,
Our shortstop is from Timbuktu.

This picture would once have seemed startling,
Exotic, unique, or unreal.
But there's been a change,
It no longer seems strange:
Where you're from isn't such a big deal.

Birthday Wish

The night before my birthday
I lie awake in bed
While thoughts about my party
Keep dancing in my head.

I think about the kids who'll come,
I think about the cake,
But most of all I think about
The wish I'd like to make.

I'd like to wish for something
That will turn out to be
A gift for everybody,
Not just a gift for me.

I'd like to wish for something
To make my mother proud,
Although she wouldn't know it
Since my wish won't be out loud.

And if I can't find words for what
I hope will come about
I'll fill my heart with gratitude—
And blow the candles out.

Growing Up

When I was eight I couldn't wait
Until I got to nine
Then ten would come soon after
As I scrambled up the line.
But when I reached eleven
I sometimes felt regret
That I was leaving childhood
Though I hadn't left it yet.

Now you may find it silly
That as a little kid
I started missing childhood
But many of us did.
And though the biggest part of me
Longed to be mature
There was another part of me
That really wasn't sure.

My way of getting over it
Is that I came to see
My parting with my childhood
Just wasn't up to me.
And having come to see this,
And grown up after all,
I'm still so glad
For the fun I had
In the days when I was small.

Poetry

When my mommy reads to me
I often ask for poetry
Because I like to hear the way
She says what poets have to say.

I mostly like the poems that rhyme,
I like the beat, and keeping time,
While making sure that I have heard
The sound of every single word.

And I've found one I like the best
That speaks to me more than the rest,
Then memorized my favorite part
So I can say it all by heart.

And should I lie awake at night
When mommy's gone and dimmed the light
I dream she's reading it to me,
And go to sleep with poetry.

Thank You

Ansie Baird, Elizabeth Barondes, Jessica Barondes, Louann Brizendine,

Katie Hafner, Cyra McFadden, Linda Pastan, Jena Pincott,

Lisa Queen, Jeanne Robertson, Susan Trott, Abby Wasserman.

Samuel Barondes began publishing poems as an undergraduate at Columbia College where he was poetry editor of *Jester*, its humor magazine. Now he does brain research and practices psychiatry at the University of California, San Francisco. These poems were first read to his grandchildren, Jonah, Ellen and Asher. He can be reached at barondes@gmail.com

Mark Wooding is an illustrator and videographer who creates online classes at the University of California, San Francisco where he is best known for short animated videos. This is his first published work. More of his work can be seen at KramGallery.com

20892003R00059

Made in the USA
San Bernardino, CA
27 April 2015